Sam
JOHNSON

WHO WAS...

Sam
JOHNSON

The wonderful word
doctor

ANDREW BILLEN

✳ SHORT BOOKS

First published in 2004 by

Short Books

15 Highbury Terrace

London N5 1UP

10 9 8 7 6 5 4 3 2 1

A CIP catalogue record for this book
is available from the British Library.

ISBN 1-904095-77-1

Printed in Great Britain by
Bookmarque Ltd, Croydon, Surrey

For Oscar and Louie

CHAPTER ONE
Dr Johnson – celebrity or lunatic?

Had you been passing through the centre of Uttoxeter, a small town in the English midlands, one gloomy October day two hundred or so years ago, you would have caught an extraordinary sight. Standing alone in the rain in the busy market place was an old man of seventy-five. He had removed not only his hat but also the wig that gentlemen of those times wore and the rain was spattering on his bare head. Great drops rolled down his vast, ugly face. There he stood for an hour to the amazement and jeers of the traders and shoppers who watched him. Perhaps he was a drunken tramp or a lunatic who had escaped his asylum.

But this man was neither poor nor mad. The sorry spectacle was Dr Samuel Johnson, one of the cleverest Englishmen who ever lived. Thanks to the thousands of words he had written and, even more, to the millions he had spoken, he was a celebrity – although, of course, in those days, long before photographs and television, celebrities were not instantly recognizable in the way they are today.

By that autumn of 1784, Sam was seriously ill. He had had a stroke the previous year and now he was suffering from asthma, indigestion, breathlessness, sweating and sleeplessness. Dropsy, the build-up of liquid in the body, had caused his legs to swell painfully. The medicine he rubbed in, which was made out of the dried bodies of Spanish flies, did him little good. Nor did the new fangled "electricity"treatment, using a machine that sent mild shocks up his arms. Sam was always complaining about his doctors – "quacks" he called them – and, although rude, he was right. It would be years before doctors had much clue how to cure people of anything. And poor Sam did not have years left.

Two months later, he was dead and ready to be

buried at Westminster Abbey near the monument to Shakespeare whose plays had fascinated and, sometimes, terrified him.

In the centuries that have passed, Sam's fame has not diminished. He was a hero to many in his day and has been a hero to many more since. There are good reasons for this, but if your idea of a hero is a brilliant footballer – fit, handsome, athletic, well-paid, stylishly dressed, with a beautiful wife and adorable children – you may have difficulty in understanding how anyone could be inspired by such a mess of a man as Samuel Johnson.

He certainly wasn't handsome. In later life he grew very fat. He was bad at sports, having been bedevilled with illnesses from childhood. And although he loved jokes, he was not, by temperament, a very happy man. He suffered terribly from depression, which then, as now, was rightly considered an illness in its own right. After his wife died thirty years before he did, leaving him with no children, he never remarried. For most of his life he was quite poor. In fact, in his late twenties he used to sign letters with the single Latin word "impransus" meaning "supper-less".

His manner was odd and, although he could speak more cleverly and amusingly than anyone before or since, he could also cause hurt with his tongue. He was extremely intelligent but he was also lazy. He had difficulty concentrating and getting down to work. He struggled to get up before noon and the longer he stayed in bed, the guiltier he felt. But he had to work whether he liked it or not. "A man may write at any time, if he will set himself doggedly to it," he once explained. He also said that only a "blockhead", that is to say a fool, would write for any reason other than to make money.

Even when he was finally able to stop worrying about money, when fortune followed fame and the King of England awarded him a pension of £300 a year in thanks for the dictionary of the English language he had spent nine years writing, he never looked well off.

He dressed appallingly. His clothes were faded and dirty and he wore his shirt collars and sleeves unbuttoned. His sooty black wig did not fit properly and, if you looked closely, you could see that it had been singed by the candles he held too close to his face when reading. His eyesight, you see, was very poor too. If you judged Sam Johnson solely by his appearance you would have been very much misled.

A famous painter of his day called William Hogarth certainly nearly was. One day Hogarth called at the home of a friend, Samuel Richardson, who was a writer of many great stories. At the window of the sitting room there stood a man shaking his head and rolling his body about "in a most ridiculous manner". Hogarth concluded he was an idiot. The poor man's family must have asked Richardson to take him in and look after him! Well, that so-called idiot was none other than the great Sam Johnson.

The odd movements observed by Hogarth were described vividly by Johnson's great friend James Boswell, who, after his death, wrote a wonderful biography of him. Pausing between sentences, Sam, Boswell recorded, made sounds like a cow chewing the cud. Sometimes he clicked his tongue against the roof of his mouth, clucking like a hen. When he had finished expressing a thought, he used to "blow out his breath like a whale". So our hero was a cow, a hen and a whale all in one. And as he spoke, his head, his arms and his body would move around. At the time, some thought he was suffering from an illness called St Vitus's Dance. Modern doctors might well have decided Sam had something known as Tourette's Syndrome and given him pills to take. Whatever it was, his unusual manner cost him jobs in his early days when he applied to teach in schools. These days, when looks are even more important, we might wonder if the greatest talker of his age would even have been allowed on television.

He would, however, surely have been a radio star. When people listened to what Sam said, rather than concentrated on how he looked, their opinions changed. That day at Richardson's house, the painter Hogarth was amazed when the "idiot" began to talk and let out a storm of complaint against the King of England, George III. He thought that God had suddenly inspired the idiot to speak.

A few years later another painter, Ozias Humphry, was introduced to Sam in his dirty little rooms off the Strand in London. Sam loved his food and concentrated on it so intently that he would stop talking and listening when he ate. The veins on his forehead would stand out and he would sweat as he chewed. That morning Sam was tossing and turning in a chair as he greedily ate his breakfast, gorging on bread and butter, slurping his tea. His stockings were down about his feet. But then he began to talk and, as Humphrey recalled, it was as though Sam were reading aloud from a book. Everything was as "correct as a second edition", the edition in which all the mistakes have been corrected.

Sam's own books have gone into many editions. He penned hundreds of articles for magazines, composed poems, translated works of Latin into English and compiled a dictionary, whose definitions have become famous. But, truth be told, only scholars read them much today. Nor would this surprise Sam. In one of his essays he imagined the earnest young scholar whose life's works would in the end be lost on the shelves of a vast library. No, what keeps Sam's memory alive are the things that he said. This is partly because, although much of his writing was worthy, solemn and somewhat depressing – in his novel, *Rasselas*, he wrote that "human life is everywhere in a state in which much is to be endured and little to be enjoyed" – his talk showed that, despite everything, he *did* enjoy life. This, after all, was a man who once said that if he had no responsibilities and no cares about the future, he would spend his life "driving briskly in a post-chaise [a small horse-drawn carriage] with a pretty woman." We can imagine how much his friends enjoyed hearing this light-hearted yet sharp-witted banter. No sooner had he said something amusing or cut someone down to size than it was all around London.

Some of his sayings remain true today. "Patriotism is the last refuge of the scoundrel," he said, for example, meaning that sometimes when politicians do not have a good argument for a policy they try to persuade everyone else to go along with it by saying what a fine country they live in and how it is everyone's duty to support it. Remember that when you next hear an American president making a speech. Equally, anyone who has faced an exam in the morning will know exactly what he meant when he said: "When a man knows he is to be hanged in a fortnight, it concentrates his mind wonderfully."

Some other statements, if they were true then, are

certainly *not* true today: "Sir," he said, "a woman preaching is like a dog walking on his hind legs. It is not done well; but you are surprised to see it done at all." Many are simply very funny put-downs, well worth saving up and using yourself when the moment arises. "Difficult do you call it, sir?" he said to a companion excusing a violinist who was struggling through a complicated piece. "I wish it were impossible."

If you got past the way he looked, the way he wriggled, and the way he insulted those he was most fond of – such as Scotsmen and actors – Sam was simply the best company in the world. He had many, many friends to prove it. And his very pampered cat, Hodge, would probably have agreed too.

CHAPTER TWO
A Difficult Beginning

What was Dr Johnson, the cleverest man in England, doing bareheaded in the rain that morning?

He was in the area because he was visiting, for the very last time, the nearby town of Lichfield, where he had been brought up. Lucy, his wife's daughter from her first marriage, whom he adored, had put him up in her comfortable house and he had enjoyed meeting old friends. But at breakfast that morning, Lucy could not find her stepfather anywhere. The servants knew only that he had left the house very early without saying where he was going. As the day wore on there was still no sign and Lucy became more and more worried.

Then, just before supper, Sam returned.

He apologised for his abrupt departure. Fifty years before, he explained, he had done something that he had regretted ever since. His father had been a book-seller and would go to Uttoxeter on market day to sell what he could. But on one occasion, the old man had been too ill to leave his bed and had asked his son to go and set up shop for him. Sam, who had recently been forced to give up university and come home to live in his parents' house, was feeling grumpy and had no intention of wasting a day selling books for a few pence in a market.

"Madam," he told Lucy, shamefaced, "my pride prevented me from doing my duty and I gave my father a refusal." So this morning, he said, he had ridden to Uttoxeter in a carriage and stood where his father, now long dead, had once stood. There he had been "exposed to the sneers of the standers-by". This was his punishment, and Sam seemed to feel much better for having endured it.

* * *

Michael Johnson was already fifty-three when his wife, who was thirteen years younger than him, had Sam, the first of their two boys. She gave birth at four in the afternoon on September 18 1709. It was a difficult labour and at first the midwife, who, rather confusingly, was a man, could not get the baby to cry and take his first breath. Not sure he would live, they decided the "poor creature" should be christened as soon as possible.

At the time Michael's books business, which included a factory that made parchment used to cover books, was doing quite well and he was well thought of in the town. But he was old to be a father for the first time and pre-occupied with his work. To Sam, as he grew up, he seemed remote and reserved.

Sarah, Sam's mother, was practical and well meaning. She came from a wealthy local family but had little in common with her husband. Towards Sam, she was sometimes over-indulgent and sometimes too quick to get cross. Occasionally she would beat him. He loved her, but did not respect her very much.

But if Sarah and Michael were not the best parents in the world, Sam was not the best son either. He did not much like being a child and looked forward to being a grown-up. He hated, for instance, having to show off his learning to relatives who treated him as if he were a dog who had been taught to sit up and beg. When they came round, he would run out and hide up a tree. He had a habit of answering back. Once his mother scolded him and called him a "puppy". Sam replied by asking her if she knew what a puppy's mother was called.

If we are to excuse him we can point out that he was not a well child. From birth he had suffered from scrofula, a disease of the glands that left him with poor sight in his left eye, deafness in his left ear and some paralysis on the left side of his face. It also gave him boils on his neck which would leave him scarred for life. In order to "cure" him he had a ridiculous operation to cut open his arm. This made a wound that was deliberately kept open for six years to let the "poisons" out. The doctors, of course, did not know what they were doing at all.

But there was one bonus from his ill health. When he was three-and-a-half his mother took him by stage-coach to London to meet Queen Anne. It may sound strange, but at the time many doctors believed that the Queen had healing hands that could cure childhood ailments, in Sam's case his scrofula. He remembered for ever this grand woman in her diamonds and long black hood, and prized the thin golden medallion she gave him, wearing it around his neck until the day he died. But he also came back with an even more important memory – of London and of the bookshop owned by one of his father's friends where they had stayed. To enter the world of books in London became young Sam's ambition.

At school, Sam excelled at his lessons, even though they were all conducted in Latin, the long-dead language of the ancient Romans. He was helped by having a very good memory. One morning, his mother gave him a passage from the Bible to learn and went up stairs about her chores. She was only half way up when she heard Sam scampering up after her. "What's the matter?" she wanted to know. He replied that nothing was the matter: he had simply already learned the passage. And, when she challenged him, he repeated it word for word.

His schooldays in Lichfield were the usual mixture

of happy and unhappy times. His first teacher, a kind man called Humphrey Hawkins, was excellent but the upper school was run by a "peevish and ill-tempered" young clergyman who took little interest in his pupils. Worse was the headmaster, John Hunter, who would flog the boys if they did not know the answer to one of his questions. Johnson later felt there was nothing wrong in whipping children if it made them work harder but Hunter was just cruel, "wrong-headedly severe", and he made Sam tremble. In fact, even the sight of Hunter's granddaughter would make him shake, because she looked so like him.

Although the cleverest boy in the school, Sam was not a swot. He put off his homework till the last minute and would make up poems and translations in his head without bothering to write them down. He did not mind helping his friends and for a while three of them would turn up at his home after breakfast to carry him to school on their backs while he dictated their homework. Although he was no good at ball games, he enjoyed swimming, rambling through the fields on the way home from school, climbing trees and jumping over stiles. He never lost his joy in these things. When as an old man he visited Lichfield three years before his death he found a railing he had vaulted over as a boy. He stared at it for a while, then laid aside his hat and wig, pulled off his coat and leapt over it. Twice.

So although he was an odd-looking boy – sickly, sometimes gloomy, always eccentric – he was popular. He was fun. He made friends at school that would last him a lifetime.

Just after his sixteenth birthday Sam made another sort of friend. He was sent to stay for a long weekend with Cornelius Ford, at Pedmore near Stourbridge, on the other side of Birmingham. Cornelius was his Uncle Joseph's son. He was already thirty-one and had been to Cambridge University which he had left to become a fashionable man about London who knew many well-known writers. He had run into debt, however, married a rich older woman and was now planning to be a vicar.

Sam found Cornelius witty, sophisticated and well read. To his surprise, Cornelius found the teenager could hold his own in conversation and was eager to learn. He was eager also to learn *how* to learn. There was no need, Sam discovered, to "turn over every leaf" but "grasp the trunk hard and you will shake all the branches". In other words, don't get lost in detail, but try to understand the general principles. In later life Johnson rarely read books all the way through. He once said there were only three books in the language that left the reader wishing they were longer than they were, and one of those was *Robinson Crusoe*.

The long weekend with Cornelius in Stourbridge turned into six months and Sam did not return home to Lichfield until the next summer. The headmaster was furious and refused to let him back to his class, so from then on Sam went to school in Stourbridge instead, though he did not enjoy that much either. It was so strict that the boys had to speak to each other in Latin, even off the school grounds, and were flogged if they were caught speaking English. He left after six months.

By now he was seventeen, well-educated and ready for university. Unfortunately, his father's business was doing badly and owed money to the taxman. Sam began work in the family bookshop, where it soon became obvious he preferred reading the books to selling them. Then, unexpectedly, a wealthy cousin of his mother's died and left her £40, which, although it does not sound all that much today, was then about what a shopkeeper or builder might earn in a whole year. She decided to use the windfall to send Sam to Oxford after all.

Oxford is a university that is made up of separate colleges, some rich, some less so, where students sleep and meet their tutors. Sam won a place at one of the poorer ones, Pembroke – not that this dampened his excitement. Father and son rode down together, his father much embarrassing him when they arrived by telling the tutors how lucky they were to have this boy genius. Fortunately, Sam, who had been sitting in silent agony, suddenly thought to quote a fifth-century Roman scholar. The professors wondered if the boastful father might not be exaggerating his son's brilliance after all.

Yet, Sam's time in Oxford was not a great success. He enjoyed the company of his fellow students. He went drinking with them and, despite his terrible eyesight, he even did his best to join in their games of cricket. It was in his studies he fell down. It was not that he did no reading, although he did not do as much as he felt he should. It was that he kept delaying writing his essays. Also, he skipped lectures. When he was fined for repeatedly failing to turn up, he complained he had been charged tuppence for something not worth a penny.

With the arrogance of most young men, Sam thought his tutor at Pembroke, William Jorden, was a "blockhead". Jorden punished him subtly by being especially nice to him, and would invite him to his rooms after dinner in the college dining hall for a glass of wine. This was designed to make Sam feel guilty, but Sam could not stop his cheekiness. One day, instead of writing the essay he had been set on Guy Fawkes, he wrote a long poem explaining why he wouldn't do it.

But while messing about at college is part of most students' lives, if messing about is all they do, the clever ones end up angry at the time they have wasted. Sure enough, Sam became bored, and then depressed. What was more, his money was running out. Far from being able to travel abroad, which he had hoped to do, he could not afford to stay at Oxford. By the end of his second autumn there, he had no money even for clothes and his big white toes stuck through the end of his shoes. The rich young men at Christ Church, over the road from Pembroke, laughed at his appearance, but when a kindly fellow student bought him a new pair of shoes and left them outside his rooms, Sam threw them away angrily.

At Christmas, he went home to Lichfield knowing he would not be returning to Oxford. He was so depressed he thought about killing himself. He was twenty, had not got his degree, and was back where he started, in his father's bookshop – and, as we know, far from happy doing what his father asked of him.

CHAPTER THREE
A poor teacher finds a
surprising wife

In December 1731, Sam's father died. He left Sam, once the family's bills had been paid, just £19. To escape work in the shop, which was now being run by his mother and younger brother, he found a job as a teacher at a school in Market Bosworth in Leicestershire.

He hated it, rowing frequently with the school's very stupid owner about his making the boys speak only Latin or Greek. He told an old school-friend that it was hard to say who had the greater difficulty – he in having to explain "nonsense" to the boys or the boys in having to try and understand it. In the end there was a terrible argument and Sam left once more for Lichfield.

In July 1733 he was turned down for yet another teaching job. Fortunately, this time a friend, Edmund Hector (or "Mund" as Sam shortened his name), came to his rescue and invited him to stay with him in Birmingham. Hector was a surgeon and had comfortable rooms near the Swan Inn, where Sam would drink far too much of a special punch known as "Bishop" made up of port, sugar and oranges. He did do some work, translating from the French a book by a Portuguese missionary to Abyssinia, but, as usual, he left things to the last minute. In the end, he dictated his translation to Hector from his bed and it was Hector who copied it out and took it to the printers. Sam was paid five guineas (a guinea being one pound and five pence) – hardly enough to live on even then, considering that even humble labourers might earn £20 a year. He went back to teaching.

In the end, over six years, Sam would teach in half a dozen schools without much success in any of them. Children found this large, bony man, more than six feet tall, with his funny walk and habit of muttering to himself frightening. Behind his back they did impressions of him. He hated teaching as much as they hated being taught. In his *Dictionary*, to explain the word "pedagogue", which is another word for teacher, he quoted some lines from a poet called John Dryden:

Few pedagogues but curse the barren chair,
Like him who hanged himself for mere despair
And poverty.

In other words, being a poor teacher was enough to make you suicidal.

* * *

Yet although he may have hated teaching, it is hard to believe that some of his pupils did not later consider themselves very lucky to have been taught by him.

Some must surely have picked up useful tips, especially those who, like him, found it difficult to sit down to serious study. His advice to young people was always to carry a book in their pockets to read when they had nothing else to do: "It has been by that means chiefly that all my knowledge has been gained." He added that "a fellow shall have a strange credit given him, if he can but recollect striking passages from a few books, keep the authors separate in his head, and bring his stock of knowledge artfully into play."

What he meant was: don't try to know everything. Learn a few things well and bring them up at the right moments. People will think you cleverer than you are.

As it turned out, Sam's worst failure as a schoolmaster was in the school he actually owned. The school was in Edial, two miles from Lichfield, and it was bought with his wife's money. Yes, Sam, who fell in and out of love easily but had enjoyed very little luck with girls, was married! His bride was Elizabeth Porter, a widow, and, at forty-five when they met, twenty years older than him.

Tetty, as he called her, had been married to a friend of his, Harry Porter, a cloth merchant in Birmingham, who died suddenly. The truth is that to begin with, Sam, by now in his mid-twenties, had been much more interested in Harry and Tetty's pretty daughter, Lucy. Lucy, eighteen at the time of her father's death, was certainly not interested back, although she was intrigued by Sam's appearance. He was, she wrote in a letter, "lean and lank so that the immense structure of bones was hideously striking to the eye, and the scars of the scrofula were deeply visible."

Lucy's mother, however, saw Sam in a different light. After one of his first visits to their house, Tetty had so enjoyed his talk that she said: "This is the most sensible man that I ever saw in my life," meaning by this not so much that he was a reasonable person but that he was capable of sensitive feeling.

Tetty, who pretended she was no more than forty, was good fun. She was plump, with big bosoms, large eyes and fine blonde hair. She was flirtatious and wore a little too much make-up, but was far from stupid. She was interested in books and liked to talk and drink, which Sam did too. Some people were later puzzled by the match, particularly as they would not always be happy together, but Sam always said it was a "love marriage". At her age, it was unlikely they would have any children but this did not mean, in those early days at least, that they did not fancy each other.

Her husband had left her six hundred pounds. Of course, her family suspected that Sam was only marrying her for her money, and while this was not so, the inheritance did allow him to set up the Edial school, or "academy", as he rather grandly called it. He started it with ambitious plans, but the school attracted only three boarders and a handful of dayboys. By the autumn of 1736, it had closed down taking several hundred pounds of Tetty's inheritance down with it. Sam soon gave teaching up for good.

The best thing about Edial was one of the older schoolboys, David Garrick, by then nineteen years old. Garrick became Sam's friend for life, although over the years they teased each other constantly. Garrick, a born actor, did a brilliant Johnson impression. Sam berated him and said anyone could be an actor if they chose; it was just a matter of remembering one's lines.

On March 2, 1737, the pair of them set off for London, each determined to make their fortune and Tetty was left behind to look after Lucy.

Garrick, whose first plan was to become a lawyer, was a small, vain man, with charm and good business sense. Sam, at twenty-seven, shared none of these characteristics. The only thing they had in common was that they both liked to talk – that and the fact they had to share a horse on their journey. This was how they travelled: One would ride on ahead; after a mile or two, he would tie up the horse at a gate and carry on walking; when he reached the gate the other would then get on it and the procedure would be repeated.

They were two poor young men and would later joke that Sam had had only tuppence ha'penny in his pocket and Garrick a penny less. In fact in Sam's pocket were also three acts of a tragic play he was working on, but it would be Garrick who within four years would be the talk of theatreland for his portrayal of Shakespeare's evil hunchback king, Richard III. His former teacher would take far, far longer to make his name.

CHAPTER FOUR
The streets of London

It was the middle of the night perhaps a year later. Two friends were walking around St James's Square, then, as today, one of the poshest parts of London. They were, as the saying goes, putting the world to rights. One, as you have guessed, was Sam, dressed in a bulky greatcoat, declaiming against the the Royal Family on the grounds that the Royal House of Hanover, which had occupied the English throne since George Louis of Hanover became George I twenty-five years before, were more German than they were British. The other was not Garrick, however. Garrick was far too busy. Having abandoned his ideas of becoming a lawyer he had started a wine merchant's business with his elder brother, but was still intent on becoming an actor. In 1741 he made his first appearance on the London stage.

No, Sam's companion was an older fellow, a shabby show-off dressed in a red cape, a wildman who had once killed a man not half a mile from where they were now strolling. His name was Savage and some thought him savage indeed. Sam was keeping odd company, and relishing it.

* * *

The reason the pair was out so late was simple. Neither had anywhere to sleep. Things had not gone well for Sam when he arrived in the capital. He had found the cheapest and smallest lodgings he could in a noisy dead-end street by the Thames and would spend no more than seven pence a night on his dinner at a café (making sure to give the waiter an extra penny as a tip). Sometimes he could not afford his rent, so he would spend the evening in a pub and then go on one of his night walks. This was not a very safe thing to do. London was not only filthy and squalid but a dangerous place to be at night. In a tremendous poem he wrote at this time, called *London*, Sam warned:

> Prepare for Death, if at Night you roam,
> And sign your Will before you sup from Home.

He was exaggerating, but London certainly had its share of child pickpockets, career thieves, kidnappers, grave robbbers, and professional killers – not to mention the old drunkard who "stabs you for a jest." Penalties were harsh. The jails were disgusting. Hangings happened all the time. If you stole more than two pounds the sentence was death. But the cruel punishments had little effect on the crime wave.

Yet Sam had also fallen in love with what he called London's "wonderful immensity". Although it covered a much smaller area than it does now, London was densely populated. It was home to some six-hundred-thousand people; one person in ten in England lived there. Sam sat in coffee houses and taverns enjoying the conversations of whoever ended up sitting next to him. Of a favourite inn, the Mitre in Fleet Street, he said there was "more learning and science within the circumference of where we sit now than in all the rest of the kingdom".

"No, sir," he added in one of his most repeated remarks, "when a man is tired of London, he is tired of life; for there is in London all that life can afford."

Sam had been told by an Irish painter he had met while in Birmingham that you could live cheaply in London. Seven and a half pence would be the weekly rent of a room in the loft (or garret). It was not somewhere you would invite people back to but if anyone asked to visit, all you had to say was that you were to be found at some coffee house or other. If you had to see someone important, go on "clean shirt days".

All this Sam found to be true enough. Nevertheless, he needed to earn something and he was not finding it easy. He visited a bookseller called Mr Wilcox, who was friends with the Garrick family, and asked to borrow five pounds. The shopowner agreed but, naturally, since he wanted his money back eventually, asked Sam how he intended to make his living.

"By my literary labours", he answered, meaning by writing. Wilcox looked back at the hulking young man and suggested he might do better as a labourer at Covent Garden market.

Before leaving Lichfield, Sam had written to a newly started paper called the *Gentleman's Magazine*, which was the first magazine to look anything like those we know today. Sam's letter had been a classic in how not to get a job. He had boasted of his own abilities while criticising the magazine's silly jokes. He expected *his* much cleverer contributions to be well rewarded. Unsurprisingly, the owner, Edward Cave, did not rush to offer him work.

Now that he was in London, however, Sam wrote again, more humbly this time, suggesting that he could translate an interesting book from Italian into English for him. Cave now sent an encouraging reply. Relieved, Sam returned to Lichfield in the late summer to bring Tetty to London and they set up home together in lodgings near what is now Oxford Street. Sam had at last finished his play, *Irene*, and read it one night in a tavern to David Garrick's brother Peter, who knew some important people in the theatre. To his disappointment, however, the manager of the Dury Lane Theatre refused even to look at it.

So once again, Sam approached Cave, a big, slow, rather humourless man, who nevertheless had an eye for what readers wanted and equally well knew talent when he saw it. Sam now offered Cave a poem he had written, praising Cave and ruthlessly attacking rival magazines.

This tactic worked much better and soon Sam was one of the *Gentleman's Magazine*'s most regular contributors, writing reviews, translations, short biographies, verse and parliamentary reports, although he only once attended a debate himself. It was in the *Gentleman's Magazine* that his long poem, *London*, was published. Sam could produce almost anything to order and at great speed, once he got down to it. He would lock his door to all but Cave's boy who would collect the pages as fast as they were written and take them to the printer.

Grub Street is the insulting name people sometimes give Fleet Street, the road where for hundreds of years London's papers and magazines were produced. Sam Johnson remains its patron saint, and the king of hacks. A "hack" is a journalist who writes quickly for money but Sam was a great hack, perhaps the greatest that journalism has ever known, for how many other hacks' hurried words are still worth reading two hundred and fifty years later? The secret is to write as if your words are *not* destined for tomorrow evening's rubbish bin, although, of course, Sam knew it was not possible for journalists to summon up that spirit every time they write. Nevertheless, a journalist need not be ashamed of his job.

Sam was earning so little money that sometimes he could not even afford a candle to write by. Nor was he getting on very well with Tetty and for periods they lived apart, she with a friend near the Tower of London and he in his lodgings in Fleet Street – if he had anywhere to sleep at all. Anyone who did not know him better would have thought this young man who stayed out so late was unmarried. In the autumn of 1739, things had got so uncertain that he left London for six months and returned north in the hope of yet again earning decent money as a schoolmaster. During this trip, in which he visited the failing family business and stayed with friends, he briefly fell in love with a bright woman his own age named Molly Aston.

In January, however, a letter arrived from London. It was from Tetty, saying that she had hurt her leg and was confined to bed. We can tell how guilty Sam felt from the letter he wrote her. He called her "my dear girl" and promised he had met no one in his "rambles" to match her. He was soon enough back in London and writing for Cave.

Sadly, Tetty's health never fully recovered and she increasingly took comfort in drink. Sam, meanwhile, decided to give up alcohol altogether, not because he did not like it but because he liked it too much. Athough he drank countless cups of tea and was fond of lemonade, for twenty years he did not have another glass. This did not stop him making the tavern as much as the coffee house his second home. "A tavern chair is the throne of human felicity," he would say. In other words, he was so happy sitting in a pub he felt like a king.

In these ale houses, Sam made the most extraordinary acquaintances. One was Samuel Boyse, the poet, who got into such debt through his drinking, that he would hand over the very clothes he was wearing to the local pawnbroker for money, first his shirt and on

41

down to his underpants. Women visitors to Cave's office, where he worked, would flee in shock at seeing one of his contributors working in the nude.

Another was George Psalmanazar, over sixty years old when Sam met him, who had for years claimed to be a native of the island of Formosa, now known as Taiwan, in the China Sea. He was paid to teach the Formosan language by Oxford University and later published a book all about the island. Alas, when the book was published abroad, it quickly became obvious to experienced travellers that he had never been there. As for the Formosan language, he had simply made it up. By the time Sam knew him his days of deceit were long behind him but by now he had become addicted to a drug called laudanum. Yet Sam called him the best man he had ever known!

And then there was the mysterious Richard Savage, Sam's night-walking companion. Like Sam, Savage was a poet on his good days and a hack on all the others. He had a long, sad face, a cheerless voice and a dignified air. He wore elegant black silk clothes, a cloak of scarlet trimmed with gold lace, and a fancy sword. However, if you looked down you would see his toes peeping through worn-out shoes. He was frequently broke and was always cadging drinks off strangers. Fortunately, his conversation was so amusing that most people were only too willing to oblige.

Savage was yet another contributor to the *Gentleman's Magazine* and it was at Cave's house they first met. He too claimed a strange history. He said he was the son of the Countess of Macclesfield, who because she had not been married to his father, Earl Rivers, had rejected him when he was a baby. First, she got him adopted by a baker's wife in Covent Garden. Then she tried to get him kidnapped and taken to America. Finally she got a shoe maker to take him on as an apprentice, hoping he would be forgotten. The Countess for years had to endure Savage's insults, blackmail attempts and his published attacks. He wrote a poem about his predicament called *The Bastard* and even broke into her house one night, leaving her screaming for help. She said his claims were nonsense and she may well have been telling the truth.

Sam, however, never for a moment doubted that Savage was who he said he was and, to be sure, he had many other distinguished supporters. The Queen was so impressed by a poem Savage had written in honour of her birthday that she promised to give him £50 a year provided he wrote her one every birthday. Gradually, however, one by one, Savage lost most of his friends through quarrelling. He unwisely even fell out with the prime minister, who had declined to keep on paying him the £50 after the Queen's death.

In 1727, some ten years before he met Sam, Savage had staggered drunk with some friends into a rough drinking den in the early hours of the morning and got into an argument with a party of people at a table they had wanted to sit at. In the brawl that followed, he thrust his sword nine inches into the belly of one of the other drinkers. At his trial he was condemned to death and was saved only by a royal pardon. Naturally, he accused his supposed mother of doing nothing to save his life. Finally, his remaining friends clubbed together to pay him a pension and he was persuaded to leave London and go and live quietly in Swansea, nearly two hundred miles away in Wales.

Sam, however, remained loyal to him. He sympathised with his faults, his moodiness, the tongue that sometimes ran away with him and the way he made fun of people he actually rather liked. All his life Sam himself felt he might be unable to resist common temptations and he would not condemn someone less able to fight them off. Besides, he saw his good points: Savage was "compassionate both by nature and principle".

When Savage died in a debtors' gaol in Bristol in 1743, Sam set about writing his biography. If it was to sell at all it would have to be topical, and one evening he stayed up all night and wrote forty-eight pages in a single sitting. The book was a magnificent defence of his dubious friend. In it he praised his courage in the bad times: "Whatever faults may be imputed to him, the virtue of *suffering well* cannot be denied him."

The book was liked – it so obviously came from the heart – but it did not make him much the richer. By now, to make ends meet, he was taking on all sorts of jobs. As well as journalism, he helped write a medical dictionary, published in weekly parts. He wrote brief lives of Sir Francis Drake, the naval captain, and of Oliver Cromwell's admiral Robert Blake.

In 1742 he was hired to catalogue the huge library

formerly owned by the Earl of Oxford, which had been bought by the bookseller Thomas Osbourne for £13,000. With almost forty thousand volumes to list, the task took him over a year. He was not pleased when, hard at work one day, Osbourne turned up accusing him of reading the books rather than listing them. Sam protested that to know what was inside a book you had to open it.

When Osbourne called him a liar, Sam grabbed the weightiest volume to hand and struck him across the head with it. Grounded by the blow, Osbourne next felt Sam's boot on his head. "Do not be in a hurry to rise," said Sam. "It will just give me the further trouble of kicking you downstairs."

So, by his mid-thirties, Sam had still not made his fortune. His play remained unperformed. Few knew his name and his hackery was paying so poorly that he could not even meet the mortgage on his mother's house in Lichfield. A plan for him to produce a new edition of Shakespeare plays had to be abandoned for legal reasons. Garrick, on the other hand, was already the famous actor he had dreamed of becoming. Sam would not have been human had he not felt envy at his former pupil's speedy success. In his darkest moments he thought of giving up writing and becoming a lawyer, although he despised lawyers as a breed.

Then, one day as he was sitting in a book shop, the bookseller happened to say that what people really needed was a dictionary of all the words in the English language. Sam's ears pricked up.

CHAPTER FIVE
Dictionary Johnson

"I believe I shall not undertake it," said Sam as if it were his last word on the subject. As we know, it certainly was not. On June 18, 1746, aged thirty-six, he signed an agreement with a group of book-sellers to compile the dictionary in return for 500 guineas – a large sum except that out of it he would need to hire assistants to help him in the mammoth task. As it turned out, even with their help, a project he had expected to take three years took nine. But this was what would make his name. By the end he would no longer be plain Sam. He would be Dictionary Johnson.

The challenge, however, was great. In bookshops today you see rows of dictionaries, but up until Sam's time they were very rare. Ever since 1476, when William Caxton set up the first English printing press, printers had spelled words as they wished, sparing children spelling tests but leading to confusion. Scholars, for instance, still sometimes wonder what word Shakespeare really meant to write.

The only half reasonable dictionary had been published back in 1721 by a Stepney schoolmaster named Nathan Bailey but it was badly flawed. It contained thousands of words but many were not in use and some of the most common ones were very poorly defined. A mouse, for instance, was simply "an animal well-known".

Sam's dictionary would not only contain proper definitions but would also explain how the words had got into the language – from Greek, Latin, Old Norse, Old French or any of the other tongues that visitors had brought with them to these islands. In addition, Sam would illustrate how a specific word was used by quoting from the works of other writers. To this day, the dictionary is as much a dictionary of quotations as it is a dictionary of meanings.

In order to be near his printers, Sam moved into a fine tall house in Gough Square, just off Fleet Street. The house, number seventeen, still stands and houses a museum devoted to his life that is a delight to visit. For the first time Sam and Tetty could afford to employ servants. In the attic Sam worked at an old table sitting on an old armchair, which, over the years would lose both a leg and an arm. Eventually, it felt like part of him. Around him sat his six assistants.

This was how they worked. Sam would look through a book by an author he admired. When he came across a passage that elegantly illustrated how a word was used he would mark it with a big lead pencil and underline the word in question. Having finished looking at the book, he would hand it to an assistant who copied out each of the marked passages on slips of paper. The slips would be arranged in alphabetical order, word by word.

Sam would then write out the meaning of the word and its etymology (or origins) on a big piece of paper and the slips containing the quotations would be pasted underneath. Friends who had leant him their books got them back with so many pencil marks that, had the scrawls been done by anyone else, they would hardly have been worth keeping.

The work was hard but it was steady and it occupied Sam's mind. He preferred to be busy. It kept dark thoughts at bay. There was also a huge sense of achievement when, at last, it was all done and the final page was sent to the printers. "I knew very well what I was undertaking – and very well how to do it – and have done it very well," he told a friend. Two thousand copies of the huge book, published in two tall volumes, were printed. In April 1755 it went on sale for four pounds and fifty pence a copy (a huge sum at the time).

In his plan for the work he said he intended to "fix the language". But languages do not stay fixed. Words come and go and those that stay change their meanings. Many of the definitions in Johnson's dictionary do not help us much today. He defines a dishwasher, for example, as the name of a bird – but then he could hardly have been expected to know that one day many homes would have a machine for washing dishes. Have you ever heard the word "deosculation"? And would you want to use it instead of the noun "kissing", which is what it means?

By the time Sam had finished his dictionary he, too, had realised that fixing a language was an impossible task. The work of a dictionary compiler – or "lexicographer" – was not to *form* but to *register* the language.

Forty-thousand words were registered in the dictionary. Although Sam was a serious scholar he could not resist paying off some old scores and risking a few jokes among the definitions. Some were against himself.

Lexicographer: A writer of dictionaries, a harmless drudge.

Some were against the Scots:

Oats: A grain which in England is generally given to horses, but in Scotland supports the people.

(Since five of his assistants were Scottish, we can imagine what they thought of that.)

Some were against the French:

Ruse: Cunning artifice; little stratagem; trick; wile; fraud; deceit; a French word neither elegant nor necessary.

And some were against his enemies, such as a certain Lord Bolingbroke.

Irony: A mode of speech in which meaning is contrary to the words as *Bolingbroke was an holy man*.

Some definitions were so convoluted that they read like jokes.

Net: Anything reticulated or decussated at equal distances, with interstices between the intersections.

And some of the definitions were just not quite right. When a lady, expecting a learned explanation, asked why he had defined "pastern" as a horse's knee rather than part of its foot, he replied: "Ignorance, madam, pure ignorance."

One of the most famous entries is that for "patron": "Commonly a wretch who supports with insolence and is paid with flattery."

There is a story behind this definition. On the advice of one of the booksellers who had commissioned the dictionary, Sam had decided to dedicate the project to Lord Chesterfield, a rich aristocrat of a literary bent.

The good lord, who was only a few years older than Sam, was flattered and, as Sam had hoped, gave him £10, not all that much compared to the cost of the scheme. But Chesterfield was not as excited about the project as its author. When Sam went to see him in his grand house, he was kept waiting in an antechamber. Sam, so the gossips said, never forgave him for this, particularly since the man he was kept waiting for was Colley Cibber, an actor and writer of whom Johnson had a very low opinion.

Chesterfield proceeded, in Sam's opinion at least, to ignore him over the long years that followed. When the dictionary was about to come out, however,

Chesterfield wrote two articles praising the accomplishment. Sam proudly refused to accept the compliment, damning it as "false and hollow". To make matters worse, he penned the earl a letter accusing him of neglect: he had brought the dictionary to the verge of publication "without one act of assistance, one word of encouragement, or one smile of favour."

Mind you, Sam added, he did not know what to expect. "I never had a patron before".

But Chesterfield had a thick skin and did not seem to mind at all, even though all of London was buzzing with how Sam had snubbed him. Chesterfield even showed the letter to friends, pointing out his favourite passages of abuse.

One of the booksellers suggested to Sam that he might have misunderstood why Chesterfield kept him waiting in his hall. If Chesterfield had known it was Sam out there he would surely have admitted him at once.

"Sir," he replied, "that is not Lord Chesterfield; he is the proudest man that ever existed."

"No, Sir," said the bookseller, "I know a prouder man that exists now. And that is yourself."

"But mine was *defensive* pride," replied Sam.

It is understandable that Sam was hurt, for the task had taken him such a very long time and the money he had been advanced had long ago run out. Some further donations would have been very welcome. Lacking them, Sam had to continue to write journalism and poetry. Perhaps reading so many other great writers for the dictionary helped, for in these years he produced some of his finest work. He launched his own magazine, *The Rambler*, almost all of it written by himself, penning its essays in the corners of the day, often with the printer's boy waiting at the door for his copy. The pieces did not ramble but they covered a range of subjects: sorrow, superstition, marriage, capital punishment, religion, writing, duty and, ironically, the uselessness of advice – "Few wander in the wrong way because they mistake it for right, but because it is more smooth and flowery."

For two years, until March 1752, *The Rambler* came out every Tuesday and Saturday.

At around this time he published his most famous poem, a long verse of nearly four-hundred lines, inspired by a Roman writer named Juvenal. *The*

Vanity of Human Wishes is as gloomy as it sounds but it was written from experience and from the heart. The first seventy lines were poured out one morning sitting up on Hampstead Hill. In one verse he imagines an enthusiastic Oxford scholar dreaming of the books he will write. Sam warns him that even if he works hard, avoids getting his heart broken by some woman and does not fall ill, he is still likely to end up poor and miserable.

Deign on the passing world to turn thine eyes,
And pause awhile from letters, to be wise;
There mark what ills the scholar's life assail,
Toil, envy, want, the patron and the jail.

As an old man he once recited this section to some friends and burst into tears.

He even managed to get his play put on and Garrick agreed to take the starring role. It ran for nine days in Drury Lane, which was by no means a disgrace, although the critics were not very kind. When later it was reported that a Mr Pot had called it "the finest tragedy of modern times" Sam's response was: "If Pot says so, Pot lies."

It was for the dictionary – although a few thought it too personal and jokey – that Sam became famous. Oxford, which he had left without completing his degree, now awarded him an honorary one. Yet its first readers must have been shocked to read its introduction. In place of triumph, there was sadness. The fact was that three years earlier Tetty had died.

Theirs had not been the happiest of marriages. She drank and took a common drug of the time named opium, which was made out of poppies. They spent time apart, with Tetty frequently going to stay in Hampstead during the long days when Sam was buried in his dictionary work. There, Sam would sometimes join her, but some nights was more interested in flirting with one of her companions, the widow Elizabeth Desmoulins.

But when Tetty fell ill for the last time, Sam nursed her tenderly. She died of opium addiction on March 17, 1752. Sam was gripped by grief.

"My distress is great," he wrote to an old friend imploring him to visit. He was too upset even to attend the funeral. Thereafter he would read only upstairs in the garret, which she had rarely visited, because every other room in Gough Square reminded him of her. He named the saucer on which his bread roll was placed every morning "Tetty" because it had once been hers.

He wrote later of the agony of being widowed. Life stops when your wife dies. Everything stands motionless. It seems as if your existence has been cut in two. Eventually, you are forced to move on. "But the time of suspense is dreadful."

Despite all the praise it received, the dictionary reminded Sam all too much of his poem about the vanity of human wishes and about how worldly success was not enough to make a person happy. He ended his preface by saying that those he had wished to please by writing the dictionary had "sunk into the grave".

"Success and miscarriage are empty sounds: I therefore dismiss it with frigid tranquillity, having little to fear or hope from censure or from praise." After all his work on the dictionary, Sam was coming very near to saying he could not care less about it.

CHAPTER SIX
The art of conversation;
the gift of friendship

Whatever else it did, the dictionary did not make Sam rich. Soon he was back editing magazines for the usual reason: money. In 1759 his mother died, and to pay for her funeral he wrote a story called *Rasselas* in the evenings of a single week.

It was about a perfectly contented foreign prince who out of misplaced curiosity travels the world trying to discover why men are generally unhappy. In the book's conclusion, "in which nothing is concluded", he returns home to his valley in Abyssinia convinced of the "insufficiency of human enjoyments". *Rasselas* would be better known, perhaps, if Jonathan Swift's slightly similar *Gulliver's Travels* had not appeared at around the same time, and had it been just a little funnier.

When he was fifty-three, the government at last recognized Sam and awarded him an annual pension of £300. He would no longer have to worry constantly about cash. In 1765, his edition of Shakespeare's plays was published and Trinity College in Dublin gave him an honorary doctorate. In middle age Sam had become Dr Johnson, the title by which the world would always remember him – although, funnily enough, he never once called himself "doctor".

* * *

Long before this title was conferred, Sam had matured from the awkward young man he was when he arrived in London into the famous figure with the lethal tongue whom people think of when the name Dr Johnson is mentioned. Way beyond London, he was famous as much for his conversation as his writing. He was the best talker in Britain. He even formed a club, The Literary Club, which met every Monday evening, just to practice the art of conversation. In the morning or, at any rate once he had hauled himself out of bed, he would receive visitors and there would be more talk until four or five in the afternoon as he and his guests drank endless cups of tea. At night he would retire to the Mitre and stay talking until very late. "Whoever," he said, "thinks of going to bed before twelve is a scoundrel."

He was more interested in winning an argument than getting at the truth. He talked for victory, but his victories were helped by knowing so much. "All knowledge is of some value," he would say, and over the years he surprised listeners by his unlikely grasp of dancing, thatching, farming, dogs, making gunpowder and much else besides. One of his friends said he had "the most knowledge in ready cash" of any man he had ever met.

He also had volumes of common sense to draw upon. Out walking with a friend, he once got into a discussion about a clever bishop's argument that things only existed in the mind. It was put to him that although the theory could hardly be true it was impossible to refute. Sam, kicked his foot hard against a large stone. "I refute it thus," he said.

But often he would attempt to justify the most outrageous prejudices or hold two contradictory views at once. He would intimidate listeners by using strange words that had turned up in his research for his dictionary. He did not mind giving offence, although he would sometimes apologise later. If he was tired of debate, he would make one final statement and conclude triumphantly: "And there's an end on't!" After one night's debate, he congratulated himself on the way home on a "good talk".

"Yes, Sir," replied his companion, "you tossed and gored several persons." Another friend complained: "There is no arguing with Johnson, for when his pistol misses fire, he knocks you down with the butt end of it."

Yet he was a good listener. He encouraged young men to speak up. He drew people out so they talked about what they knew.

His conversation was the fee he paid for company, which he craved because, as his friend the artist Joshua Reynolds noted, "solitude to him was horror": "He has often begged me to go home with him to prevent his being alone in the coach. Any company was better than none."

And what friends he had! Reynolds was the most famous portrait painter of his day and would become the first president of the Royal Academy, where his statue still stands in its forecourt today. Fourteen years younger than Sam, Reynolds was as polite and tactful as Sam was rude and awkward. Once, when Sam asked a hostess for another cup of tea, Reynolds gently reminded him that he'd had eleven already.

"Sir," Sam responded, "I did not count your glasses of wine. Why should you number up my cups of tea?" The funny thing was, Sam had no interest in painting and never looked at his friend's work. He said this was to ensure that Reynolds never read his.

They let a faintly ridiculous Irishman into their club. He was Oliver Goldsmith. At thirty-three years of age, he had already failed in his first career as a doctor and was now a hack writer. Later he would become well known for his comic novel, *The Vicar of Wakefield*, his moving poem *The Deserted Village* and his funny play, *She Stoops to Conquer*, but back then what reputation he had was for being ugly. Short, with a coarse, pockmarked face, he dressed untidily (he was following Sam's example, he said). Many thought him a poor talker.

"Sir, he knows nothing," Sam once said, but he also recognised a true fellow writer.

Edmund Burke burst into tears when he heard "Goldy" had died of a fever. Burke was to become a successful politician and a writer whose *Reflections on the Revolution in France* is still read. He was the same age as Goldsmith when he joined the club and Sam was immediately struck by his braininess. Burke, he said, was such a man that, if you met him for the first time in a street and talked to him for just five minutes you would part thinking, "This is an extraordinary man." Others complained that he was not a good listener and never told a decent joke. He did make one joke though, proving by mathematical equation that you could call Sam's friend Dr Brocklesby "Dr Rock": "Brock − b = Rock; or Brock *less* b *makes* Rock."

Dr Johnson's friends were by no means all famous. Being poor but honest was recommendation enough for Sam, who saw nothing wrong in giving money to beggars even if they spent it on drink, for why deprive the poor of their pleasures? And he loved the company of young men.

One summer's day two young admirers, Bennet Langton and Topham Beauclerk, had had one of those late nights that turn into early mornings. At three a.m. they thought it would be fun if Sam joined them on a ramble. They rapped on his door. Sam, fearing the worst, placed a little black wig on his head and flung open the door in his nightshirt brandishing a poker. Sam was reassured when he saw who it was and amused by the young men's proposal.

"I'll have a frisk with you," he said and off they went, through Covent Garden, where he helped the astonished greengrocers carry their boxes, then to a tavern, and down to the Thames where they rowed a boat to Billingsgate. "I don't like to think of myself growing old," Sam would say and, in a way, he never did.

Not all of Sam's friends were men. His homes in later years were filled with female guests and helpers: Anna Williams, who was blind; Elizabeth Desmoulins, the woman with whom he had once almost had an affair; and Poll Carmichael, a young Scottish woman who had strayed into the household one day but no one could quite remember how or why. He grew fond of a friend's daughter, Fanny Burney, a shortsighted, timid girl who had written a novel he liked full of wicked young men and filthy old women. He said she was a toad and a rogue to have written such characters and gave her great bear hugs as she gossiped with him.

But his dearest female friend was Hester Thrale. She was twenty-four when he met her and had been married for just over a year to Henry Thrale, a rich brewer. The Thrales were not in love but Henry, although rather stuffy and silent was a good man, and they liked each other. Sam first saw them in January 1765 at their town house near the brewery and then became a regular visitor to their country home at Streatham Park. Hester wrote that after his first visit they immediately invited him to come back the next Thursday, "and since then Johnson has remained to this day, our constant acquaintance, visitor, companion and friend."

Hester was from Wales and, when they met, her father was only recently dead. Perhaps she saw Sam as a kind of replacement for him. In any case, Sam was thirty-five years older than she was and, although he would flirt, there was no thought in his mind of romance.

She was short, plump, with a long neck, large grey eyes and chestnut hair. She was not a beautiful woman but he admired her liveliness, her good humour and her intelligence although her education was, he would say, that of a "schoolboy in one of the lower forms". He scolded her, rather hypocritically, for being too hard on people. He called her a rattlesnake. She called him an elephant.

They grew very close and she proved to be a very good friend, staying up with him until four in the morning when he could not sleep and listening to him when he confessed his darkest fear, that he would go mad. Sometimes he asked her to lock him up in his room for his own safety. Thanks to her, his manners and even his dress improved. He began to change his shirt and coat before, rather than after, they became smelly.

In return for her hospitality, he introduced her to his circle of distinguished company and she became a famous hostess. He also tutored her many daughters. Sam, who, of course, had no children, adored the girls and he spoiled them with sweets and played games with them. In one, their favourite, he pretended to be a giant living in a cave. One time Mr Thrale had to stop him nearly blowing up the house when he found Sam surrounded by children and servants watching the explosive results of a chemical experiment he had devised.

He was as happy staying with the Thrales as he had ever been. He called their country home his "little Paradise". There he went hunting with Mr Thrale, and ate lavishly in the evening. For a while, he even broke his habit of lying in bed all morning.

Sadly, their friendship ended badly. When her husband died after a long illness, Hester rented out their house in Streatham. Sam could now no longer stay at this place he loved. It was a blow but not nearly so great a one as her falling in love shortly afterwards with a handsome Italian singer called Gabriel Piozzi, whom she decided to marry. Her family and most of

London society were outraged that she was marrying this foreigner, a mere entertainer, so soon after her husband's death, but Sam was angriest of all. He wrote to her saying she was wrong to marry him and asked God to forgive her "wickedness". They never saw each other again and Sam could not bear to hear her name spoken.

There were other faithful friends we should not forget. A fortnight after his own wife's death, Sam had taken on a manservant called Francis Barber. Francis was black, the son of a Jamaican slave. He had been brought to England by the father of a doctor friend of Sam's and Sam had paid for his schooling in Yorkshire.

Once Francis had entered his service, Sam became very fond of him and was horrified when seven years later Frank, as he was known, ran away to sea. Having a terror of ships, which he considered floating prisons, Sam feared for Frank's life.

Fortunately, through various connections, he was able to buy him out of the navy and Frank returned, never to leave Sam again. Sam shared the view of the time that blacks were an inferior race, but he hated slavery and always treated Frank with tenderness. In his Will he left him his tortoise-shell covered watch and £70 a year (the sort of money an army officer or clergyman might earn).

And last but not least, there was Sam's cat, Hodge. One of Frank's duties was to go out to the market and buy Hodge oysters. Hodge would scramble up Sam's chest and Sam would rub his back and pull his tail. He once said, when a friend praised him, that he'd had other cats he liked better. Then he guiltily looked over to see Hodge's reaction. Imagining him to be a little put out, Sam added immediately: "But he is a very fine cat, a very fine cat indeed."

Sam loved his friends: men, women, servants and cats. When he was with them, the serious-minded writer who scolded mankind's foolishness and wickedness, became a light-hearted person, the sort who at fifty-five would swim in the cold sea at Brighton or at sixty run after a friend through Paris. Once, staying in the country, he challenged a boastful young lady to a race and, kicking his slippers into the air, beat her.

Fanny Burney wrote in her diary: "Dr Johnson has

more fun, and comical humour and love of nonsense about him than almost anybody I ever saw."

CHAPTER SEVEN
Enter Boswell

One May evening when he was fifty-three years of age, Sam happened to be in Covent Garden in London visiting one of his favourite bookshops. It was owned by Tom Davies, who when he wasn't selling books was a part-time actor. Sam did not know that on this occasion, sitting with Davies in his back parlour, was a young man who had been desperate to meet him for some time, and who was to become his most famous friend of all.

The young man was a swarthy, short, slightly plump Scotsman called James Boswell. He was twenty-two, the son of a wealthy Scottish family, the lords (or lairds as they call them in Scotland) of Auchinleck, owners of a castle in the border country just north of England. People liked him and women liked him especially. One of his good points was that he did not take himself too seriously. He once wrote a verse about himself that went:

"This maxim," he says, "you may see,
We ne'er can have corn without chaff";
So not a bent sixpence care he
Whether *with* him or *at* him you laugh.

Unfortunately, this high-spirited youth did not get along at all well with his father, Alexander, a dour Edinburgh judge who had bullied his son into following him into the law, whereas James was much more interested in books.

He would bury himself in the huge family library, one of the biggest in Scotland, and there he had discovered Sam's *Rambler* essays. A moody teenager, who had had a nervous breakdown when he was sixteen, he found in Sam's commonsensical writings much comfort and reassurance. Sam became his hero.

Boswell had once before run away from his father, riding the three hundred miles to London on horseback. Now he had his father's grudging blessing to go to London but only so that he could join the army. But Boswell was much more interested in literary fame and was determined to meet Sam. By chance he had become acquainted with Davies, the bookseller, and Boswell was delighted when he discovered that Davies and Sam Johnson were friends.

* * *

As the clumsy giant loomed towards the glass door of the shop, Boswell could hardly contain himself. "Look, my Lord, it comes," joked Davies, quoting the line from Shakespeare's *Hamlet* when the ghost appears. Boswell was very anxious to be introduced but, knowing of Sam's silly prejudice against Scotland, which he harboured even though he had never been there, begged Davies not to say where he was from.

But this is exactly what the mischievous Davies did say.

"I do indeed come from Scotland, but I cannot help it," Boswell admitted.

"That, Sir, I find, is what a very great many of your countrymen cannot help," Sam replied, making a double joke because he thought far too many Scotsmen were coming to London.

Their conversation had not started well and it did not improve when Boswell mildly joined in Sam's grumbling about his old friend Garrick who had refused to give Sam a free theatre ticket.

"Sir, I have known David Garrick longer than you have done and I know no right you have to talk to me on the subject," Sam told him. But the young Scotsman must have said something right, for when he rose to leave, he realised they had been talking for three hours.

Boswell called on him at his lodgings a few days later, and then again in three weeks. In June they met by chance in a restaurant and agreed to have supper together at the Mitre pub. There Boswell spoke from the heart about his difficult relations with his father. Sam promised that he had never believed what his father told him either.

"Give me your hand," he said, at the end of the evening. "I have taken a liking to you."

With this handshake one of the great friendships in history was established. It was not, of course, a friendship of equals. Boswell was the junior partner and looked up to Sam. He always tried to be in earshot of what Sam said even if it meant sitting right behind him.

Older friends of Sam's, such as Goldsmith, thought him a creep, and Sam himself would sometimes tire of his sucking up and having to reassure him he cared for him. But this did not stop Sam affectionately teasing him, especially about Scotland. That summer the talk at the Mitre one night turned to Scottish scenery and the country's many "noble wild prospects".

"Sir," Sam countered, looking at Boswell, "let me tell you, the noblest prospect which a Scotsman ever sees, is the high road that leads him to England."

It is sometimes thought that the two men formed an inseparable, abusive partnership like Laurel and Hardy or Blackadder and Baldrick. This is not true. Boswell was teased but he would tease back. Besides, in all the years they knew each other, they spent fewer than 300 days together. Boswell had his own life in Edinburgh, where he had a wife, to whom he was kind but not faithful, and five children, two boys and three girls. He visited England only a dozen times. But when they did meet, Boswell made the most of it. Alert to Sam's every expression and utterance, when he got back to his lodgings he would sit up entering what had been said into his journal.

Three months after they first met Boswell decided, after all, to study law and chose a university in Holland. Sam accompanied him to the docks at Harwich, where the two men vowed not to forget each other. As the ship pulled away Boswell watched Sam getting smaller and smaller on the shore, "rolling his majestic frame in his usual manner".

Boswell spent four years in Europe and on his return settled in Scotland to practise law. He allowed himself to become much too involved with those he defended, who were generally the most hopeless criminals: horse thieves, street fighters, drunken soldiers and pick-pockets.

His first criminal client was a man called John Reid whom he got off a charge of stealing a sheep. Eight years later Reid was found guilty of a similar offence and sentenced to be hanged. Boswell dreamt up a plan to cut him down from the gallows, carry him to a stables and have a doctor resuscitate him. Unfortunately, by the time Reid was carried to the stable he was, to Boswell's horror, stone dead.

It was not until 1772 that Boswell again came to stay in London, this time for eight weeks. He saw Johnson almost every day. When he returned to Scotland, to his surprise he received a letter from Sam saying he was keen to take up an offer Boswell had first made nine years before. This was for them to explore the highlands and islands of Scotland together. "Dr Johnson in Scotland," he thought, "after all he has said about my country!"

In August the following summer Sam arrived and stayed a few days at Boswell's home in Edinburgh. Boswell's wife quickly became exasperated with his endless need for tea and his frequent accidents with the candle wax. She was not very sorry when her husband and his odd friend, accompanied by a strapping Scottish servant, set off on their adventure.

An adventure it was for a man in his mid-sixties. In

the highlands, there were no roads, and therefore no coaches. The choice was between riding a horse or walking on foot. Sam wore boots and a very wide brown greatcoat with huge pockets that could have almost held the two volumes of his dictionary. In his hand, he carried a large oak stick.

He rode very well although on one occasion, on a narrow mountain path, he fell off and landed sprawling on the ground. Sam got up immediately and carried on. He was not a man prone to physical fear and when the boat they took over to one of the islands met such a storm that even the sailors shouted in terror, Sam lay calmly below on one of the bunks with a greyhound lying on his back for warmth.

Throughout the trek he was in an exceedingly good mood. When dining with a clergyman in Inverness, somehow the topic of kangaroos came up. Perhaps thinking that in such a remote part of the kingdom no one would know what they looked like, Sam stood up to imitate one, putting out his hands like feelers and gathering up the tails of his huge brown coat so as to make the animal's pouch.

To his host's astonishment, he then made two or

three vigorous bounds across the room.

They rode round Loch Ness and made west for the Highlands. Along the way they passed the heath featured in Shakespeare's great Scottish play *Macbeth*. Here three witches had told the soldier Macbeth that he would soon be king of Scotland, planting in his mind the idea that he should kill Duncan, the present king. It was an eery thought and Sam theatrically recited some lines from the play:

What are these,
So wither'd, and so wild in their attire?
That look not like the inhabitants o' the earth,
And yet are on't?

"We went on not troubled by promises of kingdoms," Sam wrote in his account of the trip. Sam pretended not to believe in ghosts and witches and such nonsense, but, having a fertile imagination, he was not immune to superstition.

He was particularly disturbed by the lack of trees in Scotland. Early in the trip he sat for an hour one afternoon by a desolate stream. "The imaginations excited by the view of an unknown and untravelled wilderness are not such as arise in the artificial solitude of parks and gardens," he noted. "The phantoms which haunt a desert are want, and misery, and danger."

On the west coast, Sam's party took a ship across choppy waters to Skye and then to Mull and Iona. Their route followed that of Bonny Prince Charlie's flight from his enemies nearly thirty years before.

The young pretender, as he was known, was from the Scottish line of kings and had attempted to regain the throne (in this sense "pretending" meant saying you were the rightful king). He was a dashing figure, and after the English defeated his army at Culloden he was sheltered by his faithful followers as he fled for France.

On the island of Skye, Sam met Flora Macdonald, now a middle-aged woman married to a gallant Highlander known as Kingsburgh. It was Flora, who, as a young woman, had helped Charlie escape the manhunt by taking him by a small open boat over the sea to Skye and then dressing him up as her maid as they rode on to safety.

"To see Mr Samuel Johnson salute Miss Flora

Macdonald was a wonderful romantic scene to me," reported Boswell.

They visited many Highland lairds, most of whom received them like princes. Sam joined in the local customs, sipping whisky as it was passed round in a shell or eating roast venison to the sound of bagpipes. But it was not only Scotland's high society he met. As they were riding past Loch Ness, the pair stopped at a little hut where an old woman was standing at the door. In the middle of the hovel was a peat fire whose smoke passed out of a small hole in the roof. At the other side of the room she kept goats. Offering her unexpected visitors a dram of whisky, she told them she was as happy as any woman in Scotland.

Back on the mainland, they made their way down the coast road to Glasgow and, after three months travelling, Sam returned to London in November. Two years later he published *A Journey to the Western Islands of Scotland*, a rather glum book in which he wrote a good deal about the scarcity of trees.

He and his guide met from time to time in the years that followed, usually in the spring when Boswell would come to stay in London for a few months. Even when apart they remained close. When Boswell wrote letters full of worry, Sam would write back telling him to visit. "Come to me, my dear Bozzy, and let us be happy as we are," he would say. "We will go again to the Mitre, and talk over old times."

CHAPTER EIGHT
A brave death; a famous life

On December 17, 1784, eleven years after their Highland jaunt, Boswell received the news he was dreading. Sam had died four days earlier at his home in London, aged seventy-five. The two had been friends for twenty-one years. Boswell was bereft.

* * *

Sam had not been well for some time. In the summer of the previous year, he had suffered a stroke during the night. A stroke, in which blood is suddenly cut off to the brain or leaks into it, causes such damage that it can leave you paralysed or even kill you. He felt it, as he told Mrs Thrale, as "a confusion and indistinct-ness" that lasted about thirty seconds. Always afraid above all of losing his mind, he tested his brain by making up a verse in Latin.

"The lines [of poetry] were not very good, but I knew them not to be very good," he said, which reas-sured him a little. But he had lost the power of speech. In the morning, he pressed a note on Frank, his servant, explaining his predicament. In a few days the famous voice returned.

He recovered somewhat over the winter and by the following April was out and about in London again, holding forth at dinner parties, being rude to bishops, staying up late at the Mitre. In June he travelled with Boswell to Oxford. Sam was in a belligerent mood, complaining about one of his fellow passengers who was knitting – in his view, "knotting", as he called it, was only a notch up from "mere idleness" – and telling the waiter at an inn that the mutton was "as bad as bad can be, ill-fed, ill-killed, ill-kept and ill-drest."

But he tired easily and friends noticed how ill he looked. Boswell feared he would not survive another

English winter and hatched a plan with a group of sympathisers to ask money from the government to send him to Italy for the winter months. At this gesture, Sam's eyes filled with tears, and he exclaimed, "God bless you all!"

The next night Sam and he parted for the last time. "Fare you well," shouted Sam as he stepped out of the carriage to make his way home. Without looking back, he sprang away with, as Boswell recalled, "a kind of pathetic briskness".

Unfortunately, the government turned down the petition and Boswell's worst fears for his friend's health proved true. Sam, who had opinions on everything, had opinions about dying too. He kept a journal in which he recorded in Latin every detail of his decline, from the medicines he took to the state of his bowels. He said he would be conquered by death but would not surrender to it. "I would give one of these legs for a year of life." But he also said: "Who can run the race with death?"

Dr Brocklesby, the subject of Burke's one recorded joke, told him it would be a miracle if he lived much longer.

"The whole of life is but keeping away the thoughts of death," Sam once said and death was always a terrible thought to him. It was not just dying. As a devout Christian he feared how his Maker would judge him: he had not read the Bible as regularly as he should have done; he had been prone to idleness; he had dishonoured his father. As for the process of dying, he claimed there was no way to prepare for it.

"It matters not how a man dies but how he lives. The act of dying is not of importance, it lasts so short a time. A man knows it must be so and submits. It will do him no good to whine."

Returning from the visit to the midlands where he stood in penance in the rain that day, he nevertheless began to prepare for the end. He made his will, leaving what little he had saved to Frank, burned piles of private letters and journals and arranged for a memorial to his parents and his brother to be placed in the church at Lichfield and another for Tetty's grave.

Gradually the energy seeped out of him. As he lay dying, he quarrelled with his doctors and complained of his male nurse: "The fellow is an idiot." The last words he spoke were to the daughter of a friend who had visited: "God bless you, my dear."

Frank and Mrs Desmoulins were in the room when his breathing became heavier and, finally, stopped.

In Edinburgh, Boswell was still stricken with grief when a letter from a publisher arrived suggesting he rush out a book about Sam. He was best placed to do so, having taken so many notes of his conversations, and there were rumours that six other "instant" biographies were in the offing, including one by Mrs Thrale who, as Mrs Piozzi, was honeymooning in Italy with her new husband.

Boswell wrote back saying that he would write a biography but he would take his time. Instead he began work on his own account of their tour of the Hebrides, *The Journal of a Tour to the Hebrides with Samuel Johnson*.

It must be said it is a far livelier account than Sam's, but then Boswell had two great subjects not just one. It begins with a beautiful sketch of Sam's contradictory personality. He was "hard to please, and easily offended; impetuous and irritable in his temper but of a most humane and benevolent heart".

"He united a most logical head with a most fertile

imagination, which gave him an extraordinary advantage in arguing." "He loved praise when it was brought to him; but was too proud to seek it." "His mind was so full of imagery that he might have been perpetually a poet."

Boswell described his physical appearance, his shaking, his poor sight and his corpulence, which approached the "gigantick". At the end he asked not to be criticised for mentioning "minute particulars": "everything relating to so great a man is worth absorbing." This became the guiding principle of the full biography that Boswell next set to work on. *The Life of Samuel Johnson* appeared, after much struggle and delay, on May 16 1791, six years after its subject's death.

It was an immediate success and remains a great portrait of a great life. In its attempt to tell the whole truth about a person it was revolutionary and did Sam no dishonour. Anyone reading it can see that Johnson's natural failings – his temper, his sluggardliness, his melancholy, his fearfulness, even his uncouthness – were part of his greatness, for he overcame these failings rather than allow them to overcome him. Thanks to Boswell's brilliant ear, we have only to open the *Life* to hear Sam talk. We may be sure Boswell tidied things up a little. It is unlikely, for instance, that Sam used "Sir" quite so often or settled quite so many arguments with "and there's an end on't". But then, on some occasions, he probably spoke even better than Boswell remembered.

Yet his talk was not uttered for posterity but to delight those with whom he shared a pot of tea or tavern table. Until the end of his life, he felt a day in which he had not made a new acquaintance was a day wasted. It was just as important not to lose touch with old friends. "To let friendship die away by negligence and silence is certainly not wise. It is voluntarily to throw away one of the greatest comforts of the weary pilgrimage."

Life for Sam was a weary pilgrimage but he knew it was best made in company. He was a big man. He had a big brain. Some said he had a big head. But his heart was the biggest part of him of all.

AN END ON'T

KEY DATES

1709: Born in Lichfield, Staffordshire, on 18th September, the son of Michael and Sarah Johnson.

1712: Taken to London for the first time to be "touched" by Queen Anne to cure his bad skin.

1717: Attends Lichfield Grammar School.

1728: Joins Oxford University.

1729: His money runs out and he leaves. Over the next few years takes various lowly teaching jobs.

1731: Father dies.

1735: Marries Tetty Porter.

1737: Rides to London with his former pupil and friend David Garrick; begins a long period scratching a living from journalism.

1743: His strange friend Richard Savage dies.

1744: His *Life of Savage* is published.

1746: Agrees to write a dictionary of the English language.

1749: Publishes his great poem *The Vanity of Human Wishes*.

1750: Begins a new magazine, *The Rambler*.

1752: Tetty dies.

1755: His dictionary is finally published.

1759: His mother dies; writes *Rasselas* to pay for her funeral.

1762: A yearly grant from the government finally ends his financial worries.

1763: Is introduced to James Boswell.

1765: Meets Mrs Thrale.

1773: Tours Scotland with Boswell.

1779: *Lives of the Poets* comes out.

1783: Recovers from a stroke.

1784: Dies in London on December 13 aged 75.

AUTHOR BIOGRAPHY

Andrew Billen lives in London. He is a journalist who has worked for *The Observer*, the *London Evening Standard* and *The Times* where he writes a weekly interview. He has interviewed hundreds of interesting people but none as interesting as Sam Johnson.

OTHER TITLES IN THE **WHO WAS...** SERIES

Kate Hubbard
1-904095-80-1

Ned Kelly
Gangster hero of the Australian outback
Charlie Boxer
1-904095-61-5

William Shakespeare
The mystery of the world's greatest playwright
Rupert Christiansen
1-904095-81-X

Queen Victoria
The woman who ruled the world
Kate Hubbard
1-904095-82-2

Florence Nightingale
The lady with the lamp
Charlotte Moore
1-904095-83-6

Madame Tussaud
Waxwork queen of the French Revolution
Tony Thorne
1-904095-85-2

Nelson Mandela
The prisoner who gave the world hope
Adrian Hadland
1-904095-86-0

The Bloody Baron
Evil invader of the East
Nick Middleton
1-904095-87-9